GLASGOW &
SOUTH WESTERN
AND OTHER STEAMERS

GLASGOW &
SOUTH WESTERN
AND OTHER STEAMERS

Alistair Deayton

TEMPUS

Acknowledgements

The photographs in this book have, in the main, been collected by myself over a period of some thirty-five years or so. Many were issued by the Clyde River Steamer Club for sale at their monthly meetings.

My special thanks go to Iain Quinn; Robin Boyd; Archie McCallum, for material from the Clyde River Steamer Club archives; Bruce Peter, for photographs from the collection of his grandfather, A. Ernest Glen; The Glasgow Room, Mitchell Library, North Street, Glasgow, for permission to use illustrations from the Graham Langmuir Collection.

Published sources used for the captions have been many. The majority of the basic information comes from Duckworth and Langmuir's 'Clyde River and Other Steamers'. Much other detail has come from articles published in the CRSC's annual magazine 'Clyde Steamers' over the past almost forty years. My thanks go to Iain Quinn, as always, for checking the proofs for factual errors and adding helpful suggestions for the location of certain illustrations.

First published 2002
Copyright © Alistair Deaton, 2002

PUBLISHED IN THE UNITED KINGDOM BY:
Tempus Publishing Ltd
The Mill, Brimscombe Port
Stroud, Gloucestershire GL5 2QG
www.tempus-publihing.com

ISBN 0 7524 2773 3

TYPESETTING AND ORIGINATION BY
Tempus Publishing Limited
PRINTED IN GREAT BRITAIN BY
Midway Colour Print, Wiltshire

Contents

Introduction

Glasgow & South Western Railway

In December 1869 the Greenock & Ayrshire Railway reached Greenock Princes Pier. This company was taken over by the Glasgow & South Western Railway in 1872. Two further railheads were established by the GSWR, with branches off the Kilwinning to Largs branch, Fairlie Pier, in 1882 and Ardrossan Winton Pier as early as 1840.

The Greenock & Ayrshire Railway briefly operated the steamers *Athole* and *Craigrownie* in 1870, but that was not a success.

In 1891 the GSWR applied for parliamentary powers to operate its own steamers, and was thus the third of the Clyde Coast railway companies to commence operation in earnest, following the NBR in 1882 and the CR in 1889.

The GSWR appointed Alexander Williamson as Marine Superintendent and the first four steamers were purchased in August 1891 from his father, Alexander Williamson (Senior). These were the 'Turkish Fleet' of, *Sultan, Sultana, Viceroy* and *Marquis of Bute*. In the same year *Chancellor* was purchased from the Lochgoil & Lochlong Steamboat Co. Ltd, and *Scotia* from Capt. Buchanan.

The following year the first three steamers to be built for the company appeared, *Neptune* and *Mercury* from Napier, Shanks & Bell, and the beautiful two-funnelled *Glen Sannox*, for the Ardrossan to Arran service, from J&G Thomson.

In 1893 a smaller pair of sisters were built, *Minerva* and *Glen Rosa*, both from J&G Thomson. As the 1890s progressed, another steamer was built by J&G Thomson, *Jupiter*, for the excursion trade.

In 1898 a paddle steamer was purchased which was partly built, but on which the payments had not been forthcoming from the Thames company for which she had been ordered. This was *Juno*, which was placed in the day excursion trade out of Ayr.

1902 saw the arrival of the final paddle steamer to be built for the fleet, *Mars*, built by John Brown at Clydebank, who had taken the yard over from J&G Thomson.

In 1904, a paddle steamer was purchased which had been built for Capt. John Williamson, but had been sold on the stocks to South of England owners. She had been intended to be named *Kylemore*, but had served on the South Coast as *Britannia*, and entered the GSWR fleet as *Vulcan*.

Opposite: Marquis of Bute, one of the six steamers purchased by the GSWR in autumn 1891 to start their Clyde steamer services.

In 1906 John Brown's had available an experimental set of turbine machinery, which had been built as a model for that fitted in Cunard's *Carmania*. A hull was built around this and it became the GSWR's only turbine steamer, *Atalanta*.

Gradually the second-hand purchases had been sold; *Sultan* and *Scotia* in 1893, *Sultana* in 1897, *Chancellor* in 1901, *Marquis of Bute* in 1904, *Viceroy* in 1907 and *Vulcan* in 1908.

In 1907 the wasteful competition, which had been a feature of the earlier years of the decade, was halted with a joint operating agreement between the GSWR and the CSP.

The First World War saw the requisitioning of the entire fleet, mainly for minesweeping, and the loss of two steamers, *Neptune* in 1917 and *Mars* a week after the armistice. In addition, *Minerva*, which had been on duty in the eastern Mediterranean, was sold there after the war and never returned to the UK.

1923 saw the great Amalgamation of Railway Companies throughout the UK. Both the Caledonian and the Glasgow & South Western became part of the London Midland & Scottish Railway.

The GSWR steamers had always had a very distinctive colour scheme of dove grey hull and red black-topped funnel, arguably the most beautiful of the old Clyde steamer liveries. After absorption into the LMS fleet, they retained the grey hulls for 1923, but these were repainted black in 1924. Both 1923 and 1924 saw the 'tartan lum' funnel colours of yellow with a red band and black top. In 1925 they sailed in the full LMS colours. The ex-GSWR steamers were actually owned by the LMSR until 1938, when the last survivor, *Glen Rosa*, was transferred to CSP ownership.

1924 saw the withdrawal and scrapping of *Glen Sannox*, which required a new boiler. *Juno* was withdrawn in 1931, *Mercury* in 1933, *Jupiter* in 1935, *Atalanta* in 1936 and *Glen Rosa* in 1939. Of these, only *Atalanta* was sold for further service, the others being sold for scrap.

Atalanta was sold for service at Blackpool and was used as a netlayer in the Second World War, only being scrapped in 1947. Thus passed the final GSWR passenger steamer, although the paddle tug *Troon* lasted a further year.

The Campbeltown & Glasgow Steam Packet Joint Stock Co. Ltd

The Campbeltown & Glasgow company dated back to the early years of steamboat services on the Firth of Clyde, starting operations in 1826. Early paddle steamers used were *Duke of Lancaster* (1826-1845), *St Kiaran* (1835-1848), *Duke of Cornwall* (1842-1866), *Celt* (1848-1868) and *Druid* (1857-1868). In 1867 the fine two-funnelled saloon steamer *Gael* was built for the day excursion trade to Campbeltown from Greenock.

The following year the screw steamer *Kintyre* joined the fleet, with the similar *Kinloch* appearing in 1878. In 1885 *Davaar* replaced *Gael* on the day excursion trade. *Kintyre* and *Kinloch* carried on with a daily single service in each direction from Glasgow to Campbeltown with calls at Greenock, Lochranza, and Carradale, and ferry calls at Pirnmill and Saddell. On 18 September 1907 *Kintyre* was run down and sunk off Skelmorlie by the Union S.S. of New Zealand's new *Maori* whilst the latter was on trials, and was replaced on the main service by *Davaar*. In 1926 *Kinloch* was withdrawn and replaced by the new *Dalriada*.

On 4 March 1937 the Campbeltown & Glasgow steamers were amalgamated with Clyde Cargo Steamers. On the 9th of that month, the combined company was known as Clyde & Campbeltown Shipping Co. Ltd, the majority of the shares being owned by David MacBrayne Ltd. The combined company changed the old funnel colours to those of Macbrayne, red with a black top, but kept its name and house flags.

The passenger service continued into the early months of the Second World War, and ceased on 16 March 1940. *Davaar* was sent to Newhaven where she was kept with steam up for use as a blockship in the event of a German invasion. *Dalriada* was in collision with a destroyer in

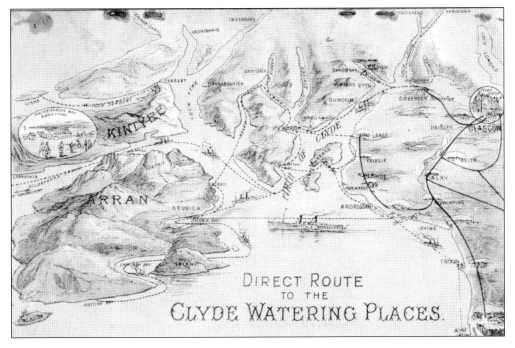

The GSWR stylised map from the August 1901 timetable.

early 1940, was repaired at Greenock, and was then laid up in the East India Harbour until she went to the Thames as a salvage vessel in April 1942, and sank there in June of that year after hitting a magnetic mine.

Clyde Cargo Steamers Ltd

Clyde Cargo Steamers Ltd was formed in 1917 by the merger of Hill & Co. and the Minard Castle Shipping Co. Ltd, along with interests of John Williamson & Co. and David MacBrayne Ltd. The company provided cargo sailings to the Clyde Islands and isolated parts of the mainland, an essential service before the car ferry and improved roads on the mainland.

Hill & Co. had started steamer service in 1879 with the small screw cargo steamers *Success* and *Bute*. In 1882 they added the paddle steamer *Cumbrae* to provide a passenger service from Fairlie to Millport, and she was joined the following year by *Arran*. This service ceased after the GSWR introduced their own steamers on the route in 1891. In 1890 the screw steamer *Bute No.2* was introduced, offering a passenger and cargo service for a year or so. In 1892 a third *Bute* was launched and in 1898 *Bute No.4* replaced her. In 1912 the former yacht *Barmore* was purchased and converted to the cargo steamer *Arran*.

The Lochfyne & Glasgow S.P. Co. operated a cargo service from Glasgow to Inveraray with *Minard Castle*, which had been built for the company in 1882. In summer 1889 a passenger service was operated from Kingston Dock to Ardrishaig via Skipness with *Sultana*, purchased from Capt. John Williamson, but this lasted only one season. In 1913 *Minard Castle* was taken over by R.G. Campbell and shortly afterwards registered in the name of the Minard Castle Shipping Co. Ltd.

Clyde Cargo Steamers acquired MacBrayne's *Lapwing* in 1918. Around 1920 she was converted to a pure cargo ship, and in 1926 was renamed *Cowal*. In 1924 the trawler *Jane* was purchased for an express service to Rothesay, but only lasted two years in the fleet. *Lintie* was purchased in 1925 for a Holy Loch cargo run. A third, *Arran,* was built for the company in 1926 but was wrecked on Barmore Island in January 1933. In 1926 *Minard* was also built, and in 1928 her sister *Ardyne.* 1933 saw the building of the final steamer for Clyde Cargo Steamers Ltd, a fourth *Arran.*

Following the formation of the Clyde & Campbeltown Shipping Co. Ltd, the fish-carrying steamer *Marie* was purchased in 1939 and, in 1945 and 1946 the motor vessel *Empire Tulip* was chartered for the Campbeltown cargo service.

In 1949 the Clyde & Campbeltown Shipping Co. Ltd was nationalised, becoming part of the Railway Executive. By this time only three steamers survived in service, *Minard, Ardyne* and *Arran.* The latter was renamed *Kildonan* in 1952 to free the name for the new car ferry. The car ferries made the cargo steamers redundant and *Minard* was withdrawn in autumn 1954, *Ardyne* in 1955 and *Kildonan* on the advent of *Glen Sannox* in 1957. The black funnel colours of Clyde Cargo Steamers were changed to red with a black top in 1937, and yellow with a black top in October 1949

Other Operators

There have been only a handful of steamers used on the Clyde (at least in the photographic era since around 1890) which were never owned by the railway companies or companies such as Williamson & Buchanan, which were later absorbed by the railway companies.

These included *Adela* and *Victoria* from Gillies & Campbell's Wemyss Bay fleet, the big *Culzean Castle* which ran rather unsuccessfully on the Campbeltown run, the tiny *Fairy* on the Inveraray to St Catherine's crossing, and *Ailsa* and *Lady Ailsa*, the steamers that ran from Girvan to Ailsa Craig. In later years there were the motor launches *Gay Queen*, *May Queen* and *Maid of Bute* operating from Rothesay and *Taransay* and *Wimaisia* of 1948 with another abortive service to Campbeltown. Bringing the story up to date are the vessels of Clyde Marine Motoring, including *Rover*, *The Second Snark*, *Kenilworth* and *Cruiser. The Second Snark* has recently reintroduced scheduled calls at Lochranza. Early plans are in place to rebuild Lochranza Pier for the 2003 summer season, although not on the same scale as when last used in 1973.

Other small motor vessels used on the Firth of Clyde, although not illustrated in this volume were *Cramond Brig* which operated a Largs to Millport service in the 1930s, *Viking Saga* of Arrochar Boat Hiring, *Granny Kempock*, *Lady Jane Ritchie*, *Westering Home*, *Gourockian* ex Ashton, *Countess of Kempock*, and *St Gerrans*, all operating out of Gourock, and the small open boats running trips from the beach at Largs and Millport.

One
Glasgow & South Western Railway Steamers

Athole is seen here in 1885 across the end of Rothesay pier, with *Columba* arriving and *Adela* at the far end of the pier. Barclay Curle had built *Athole* in 1866 for Capt. Duncan Stewart's Glasgow to Rothesay service. In 1870 she was sold to the Greenock & Ayrshire Railway for a Greenock to Kilmun and Rothesay service but this was short-lived. (*CRSC archive*)

Athole in mid-firth. In 1882, by which time she was back on the Broomielaw to Rothesay service, she was sold to Capt. Sandy McLean, in 1888 she was sold to the Bute Steam Packet Co., and in 1897 to Capt. James Williamson. She was scrapped shortly after, probably never running under his ownership.

Craigrownie was built in 1870 by R. Duncan & Co. of Port Glasgow with a single cylinder oscillating engine by Rankine & Blackmore for Brymner & Co.'s Greenock to Kilmun service. She was sold to the Greenock & Ayrshire Railway to run along with *Athole*, but later that year was sold to the Thames where she ran as *Duke of Edinburgh* until sold to French owners in 1897. In 1899 she was broken up. The above is from a negative from the Langmuir collection entitled *Craigrownie*. The steamers at the Broomielaw are *Ardencaple* and Buchanan's *Eagle* of 1864. The name on the first bow to be seen, that is the third ship from the photographer, appears to be *Craigrownie*. Note that this picture was taken in 1870; the bridge into Central Station was not built until 1879. *(G.E. Langmuir Collection, Mitchell Library)*

The three steamers of the Turkish Fleet, owned by Capt. Alexander Williamson, seen at Port Bannatyne in the 1880s. From left to right, *Viceroy*, *Sultan* and *Sultana* (N.B. named after the wife of a sultan). This is an early morning specially posed photo.

Sultan was the oldest of the four steamers purchased from Capt. Alexander Williamson (Senior) by the GSWR in 1891. She had been built in 1861 by Barclay Curle, with single cylinder machinery from *Wellington* of 1853 constructed by J. Barr, for the McKellar fleet for the Glasgow to Kilmun service, but was sold to Captain Williamson after only a year and used on the Rothesay and Kyles of Bute service. She is seen here in Williamson colours, racing *Chancellor*. (*CRSC archive*)

Sultan was purchased by the GSWR in September 1891. In April 1893, surpassed by the newly built GSWR steamers, she was sold to Capt. John Williamson, who renamed her *Ardmore*. (*A. Ernest Glen collection*)

In September 1894 *Ardmore* was sold to David MacBrayne who renamed her *Gairlochy*, and placed her on the Caledonian Canal service from Inverness to Banavie. An aft deck saloon was added and she was shortened by 18ft to fit the canal locks. She continued on this service until burnt out and sunk at Fort Augustus in November 1919. Her remains can still be seen beneath the surface of Loch Ness. She is seen here entering the locks at Fort Augustus.

Sultana had been built in 1868 by Robertson & Co. of Greenock, with a single diagonal engine by W. King & Co., for Capt. Williamson, in whose colours she is seen here.

Sultana in GSWR colours. The railway company purchased her in August 1891 and she operated during the 1892 summer on the Fairlie to Millport crossing, and in 1893 to the Holy Loch. She also served on the Rothesay service. In March 1897 she was sold to Capt. John Williamson.

Another view of *Sultana*, this time with her aft saloon windows winter-boarded. (*A. Ernest Glen collection*)

In August 1896, following the arrival of *Jupiter* in the GSWR fleet, *Sultana* was sold to Capt. John Williamson, and in 1899 to the Lochfyne & Glasgow S.P. Co. for whom in that season she operated a passenger/cargo service from Glasgow Kingston Dock to Ardrishaig via Dunoon, Fairlie, Millport, Skipness and Tarbert. In March 1900 she was sold to owners at Cherbourg, and was broken up around 1907. She is seen here in 1898 in John Williamson's colours with the white black-topped funnel introduced in that year, and white paddle boxes.

Marquis of Bute was also being built in 1868, but by Barclay Curle. She was built for Capt. Sandy MacLean. From 1869 she provided rail-connected services at Greenock's Princes Pier and on 7 April 1887 was the first steamer to call at Gourock Pier, then still unfinished. Capt. Alexander Williamson acquired her in 1889, and she is seen here in his colours.

Marquis of Bute was purchased by the GSWR in September 1891, and spent from 1893 to 1895 on the Fairlie to Millport service, replacing Hill & Co.'s *Cumbrae*. She is seen here at Fairlie.

Marquis of Bute at Greenock's Princes Pier showing the new Italianate pier buildings opened in 1894. Off the pier is *Windsor Castle* of 1875 of the Lochgoil Co. At the far end of the pier is an NB steamer.

Marquis of Bute racing away on a teatime commuter departure from Princes Pier, with *Chancellor* in the background. *(A. Ernest Glen collection)*

A couple of minutes later. *Neptune* is now coming up to pass *Marquis of Bute* and *Chancellor* has gained some ground. *Marquis of Bute* was sold in May 1904 to Capt. John Williamson, who used her on a service from Belfast to Bangor. In 1906 she was sold to an owner at Newry and the following year to a Preston owner. She was broken up in 1908.

Viceroy was the third of the 'Turkish Fleet' and had been built in 1875 by D&W Henderson Ltd with single-cylinder diagonal machinery by Hutson & Corbett. In 1886 she was re-boilered and two years later her engine was converted to a two-cylinder version. Around that time she was lengthened and fitted with an aft deck saloon and a small fore deck saloon. In 1892 the GSWR ran *Viceroy* in a trial livery of black hull for a short period before they decided on their standard livery of dove grey hull and white paddle boxes. *(A. Ernest Glen collection)*

Passengers disembarking from *Viceroy*. Note the male head apparel then considered *de rigeur* for a trip to the coast. A sailor is about to empty a sack of coal into the bunkers. Note the open cover by his feet.

Viceroy in full GSWR livery departing from Cove Pier. From 1896 until 1903 she was the main steamer on the Fairlie to Millport run.

Viceroy, seen here arriving at Greenock Princes Pier, remained in the fleet until sold in 1907 to the Mersey Trading Co. Ltd.

This company renamed her *Rhos Colwyn*, replacing the previous steamer of that name, formerly *Tantallon Castle* on the Forth. She offered excursions from Liverpool to Colwyn Bay, Llandudno and Beumaris or Caernarvon in the 1907 and 1908 summer seasons. At the end of the 1908 season, the Mersey Trading Co. went out of business. In November 1908 she was sold to an owner at Rhyl and was scrapped in 1911.

As well as the four steamers purchased from Capt. Alexander Williamson in 1891, an additional two were purchased by the GSWR to get its initial services running in 1892. One of these was *Chancellor*, purchased from the Lochgoil & Lochlong Steamboat Co. Robert Chambers Jr. of Dumbarton had built her in 1880 for The Lochlong & Lochlomond Steamboat Co.'s service from Helensburgh and Greenock to Arrochar, connecting with the Loch Lomond steamers. She had two-cylinder simple diagonal machinery by Matthew Paul. She was sold to the Lochgoil & Lochlong Steamboat Co. in 1885, and iis seen here off Greenock in their colours.

Chancellor was initially chartered by the GSWR from 18 May 1891, and was purchased by them on 21 July of that year after their steamer-owning Act of Parliament had been passed. In the winter of 1891-2 *Chancellor* was reboilered and had her engines compounded by Blackwood and Gordon. She remained on the Lochgoilhead service with some runs to the Holy Loch piers and Blairmore. (*A. Ernest Glen collection*)

In April 1901 *Chancellor* was sold to a company at Ferrol in Spain, where she ran as *Comercio* until converted to a coaling barge in 1911.

The sixth steamer to be purchased in 1891 was *Scotia*, along with the goodwill of the Ardrossan to Arran service. She had been built in 1880 by H. McIntyre & Co. at Paisley, with two-cylinder double steeple machinery by William King & Co., for Capt. William Buchanan's Glasgow to Rothesay service. She is seen here leaving the Broomielaw between 1880 and 1883 with *Vivid* behind her. In 1887 she was transferred to the Ardrossan to Arran run; a raised focsle had been added in the previous year to make suitable for this service in exposed waters.

Scotia continued on the Ardrossan to Arran service until replaced by the first of the new steamers, *Neptune*, in April 1892. She received new boilers and new wider funnels then, and spent the summer of 1892 offering excursions from Ayr. (*A. Ernest Glen collection*)

Scotia arriving at Brodick. In 1893 she was sold to Edwards, Robertson & Co. of Cardiff.

Scotia served Edwards, Robertson & Co. until the end of the 1895 season. She is seen here in their colours departing from Penarth. After they went under in 1895, she was owned by John Gunn. After he went out of business in 1899 she was purchased by P&A Campbell who operated her until 1903 when she was sold to Italian owners for service from Naples to Sorrento and Capri.

Scotia was initially owned by the Soc. de Nav. della Peninsula Sorrentino, along with *Lady Rowena* and Campbell's *Princess May*, and was renamed *Principessa Mafalda*. In 1906 she was sold to the Soc. Napoletana di Navigazione a Vapore and renamed *Epomeo*. This became the Compania Napoletana di Navigazione a Vapore in 1910, and she was sold in May 1912 to Tomaso Astartito of Naples who used her as a cargo ship. She was scrapped at Baia a year later. Many publications state that she was sunk by a mine in 1914, but Italy did not enter the war until May 1915.

Neptune was the first steamer to be built for the GSWR, coming from Napier, Shanks & Bell at Yoker on the site of today's Rothesay Dock. She started a theme of naming steamers after Roman deities and, in fact, apart from the two steamers named after Arran Glens, this theme was followed until the last GSWR steamer, *Atalanta*. *Neptune* had what was by now conventional two-cylinder, compound, diagonal machinery by David Rowan & Co. She entered service on 13 April 1892 on the Ardrossan to Arran route, but in June of that year was replaced there by *Glen Sannox*, and operated out of Princes Pier to the Kyles along with *Mercury* for that, and the following, summer season's service.

Neptune at Greenock Princes Pier. In 1894 and 1895 she ran to Arran via the Kyles in competition with *Ivanhoe*, that service having been taken over from Capt. Buchanan in the former year, and from July 1896 operated the Ayr excursion. In 1897 *Neptune* added a weekly day excursion from the upper firth to Stranraer.

Neptune arriving at Ayr in a postcard view. She continued on the Ayr excursions until the arrival of *Juno* in 1898, after which she operated an excursion programme from Princes Pier. From 1902 this was altered to a daily excursion to Ayr, except Thursdays when she sailed to Stranraer.

NEW POPULAR EXCURSIONS
BY SALOON STEAMER
"NEPTUNE" or "JUPITER."
(WEATHER PERMITTING.)

To STRANRAER
(Passing Ailsa Craig en route)
On THURSDAYS.
(Withdrawn after 5th September.)
Train from St. Enoch, 7-45 ; Paisley (Gilmour Street), 8-2 a.m.

			a.m.
Princes Pier,	Steamer dep.		8 45
Kirn,			9 5
Dunoon,			9 10
Innellan,			9 25
Rothesay,			9 45
Craigmore,			9 50
Largs,			10 20
Millport { Keppel Pier,			10 35
Millport { Old Pier,			10 40
Stranraer,		arrive abt.	2 10p

			p.m.
Stranraer,	Steamer dep.		3 15
Millport { Old Pier,			6 30
Millport { Keppel Pier,			6 35
Largs,			6 50
Craigmore,			7 15
Rothesay,			7 20
Innellan,			7 40
Dunoon,			7 55
Kirn,			8 0
Princes Pier,		arr.	8 25
		Train dep.	8 30

RETURN FARES.

	1st Cl. & Cab.	3rd Cl. & Cab.	3rd Cl. & Stg.
From Glasgow or Paisley to Stranraer,	6/6	5/6	4/6

	Cabin.	Steerage.
From Greenock, Kirn, and Dunoon to Stranraer,	*4/	*3/
From Innellan, Rothesay, Largs, or Millport,	*3/	*2/

*VALID ON DAY OF ISSUE ONLY.

NEW CIRCULAR TOUR.

From Glasgow or Paisley to Stranraer by Steamer and back by Rail, **or** vice versa.

Fare for the Round, ... 3rd Class and Cabin, **7/6***

NOTE.—Tickets for this Tour are also issued on board Steamer from Greenock at same fare.

*Valid on day of issue only.

The timetable for the excursion to Stranraer in August 1901, advertised by *Neptune* or *Jupiter*.

Around 1908, the forward end of *Neptune's* fore deck saloon was plated in, although some publications have erroneously stated that this was done in 1897 for the commencement of the Stranraer sailings. In 1907 and 1908 *Atalanta* had been the Greenock to Ayr excursion steamer.

Neptune heading out of Rothesay. From 1909 she was mainly employed on the Arrochar excursion run and an afternoon run to the Kyles of Bute.

Neptune at Rothesay pier. On the outbreak of the First World War she initially served on the Lochgoil run, and later from Ardrossan to Arran. In January 1916 she was requisitioned as the minesweeper HMS *Nepaulin*. On 20 April 1917 she sank after hitting a mine off Dunkirk.

Glen Sannox entered service on 6 June 1892. She was built by J&G Thomson of Clydebank and was designed to compete with the CSP's flyer *Duchess of Hamilton* on the Ardrossan to Arran run. With her two funnels and promenade deck plated to the bow, she was one of the most powerful of Clyde Steamers and, having reached a speed of 20.25knots on trials. She was the first to have the main deck plated in up to the bow and had the largest paddle box crest, featuring the GSWR logo, of any Clyde paddle steamer. (*A. Ernest Glen collection*)

Glen Sannox off Mount Stuart on the eastern coast of Bute on her VIP cruise on 4 June 1892, her first day with passengers.

Glen Sannox at Brodick pier. On her first crossing her time from Ardrossan to Brodick was only thirty-three minutes. (*CRSC archive*)

Glen Sannox served the three Arran piers of Brodick, Lamlash and Whiting Bay, and also made a ferry call at Kings Cross between the latter two piers, where she is seen here.

Glen Sannox at Whiting Bay Pier. From 1892 until the construction of the pier in 1899, this had been a ferry call like the one at King's Cross. In her early seasons she also offered a variety of cruises from the Arran piers during the time in the middle of the day when she would otherwise be lying idle there. On Mondays and Wednesdays she sailed round Arran, on Tuesdays and Thursdays round Ailsa Craig, and on Fridays to Campbeltown Loch. (*A. Ernest Glen collection*)

Glen Sannox featured on the cover of the GSWR summer programmes, in this case that for August 1901.

POPULAR DAILY EXCURSIONS

By Saloon Steamer "GLEN SANNOX,"
Via ARDROSSAN,

To the ISLAND OF ARRAN

TRAIN LEAVES GLASGOW (ST. ENOCH) AT 9-10 A.M.
      ,,   ,,   PAISLEY (Gilmour St.) AT 9-24 A.M.

Steamer leaves Ardrossan at 10-0 a.m., calling at Brodick, Lamlash, King's Cross, and Whiting Bay.

The "Glen Sannox" returns from Whiting Bay at 3-10 p.m.; King's Cross, 3-20 p.m.; Lamlash, 3-35; Brodick, 4-0 p.m. (except Saturdays.) *For Saturday Sailings, see page 6.*

RETURN FARES.

From **GLASGOW** and **PAISLEY**, 1st Cl. and Cab., **5/6**; 3rd Cl. and Cab., **3/9**
  ,, **ARDROSSAN**, ...   Cabin, **2/**;   Steerage, **1/6**
  ,,   ,,   Saturdays only,   ,, ***1/9**;   ,, ***1/3**

*Valid on day of issue only.

Tickets are also issued from other G. & S.-W. Stations.

POPULAR MID-DAY EXCURSIONS

By Saloon Steamer "GLEN SANNOX"
(Weather favourable).

(Withdrawn after 6th September.)

TRAIN LEAVES ST. ENOCH AT 9-10 A.M.

Steamer leaves Ardrossan at 10-0 a.m.; Brodick, 10-38 a.m.; Lamlash, 11-0 a.m.; King's Cross, 11-5 a.m.; and Whiting Bay, 11-15 a.m.; thence

On MONDAYS, WEDNESDAYS, and FRIDAYS
(Except 2nd August),

Round the ISLAND OF ARRAN.

On TUESDAYS,

Round AILSA CRAIG.

On THURSDAYS (except 1st August),

To CAMPBELTOWN LOCH.

RETURN FARES.

From **GLASGOW** and **PAISLEY**, 1st Cl. and Cab., **6/6**; 3rd Cl. and Cab., **5/**
  ,, **ARDROSSAN**, ...   Cabin, **3/**;   Steerage, **2/**
  ,, **ARRAN PORTS**, ...   ,,   **2/**;   ,,   **1/6**

This August 1901 timetable offered these excursions by *Glen Sannox.*

The two-cylinder, compound, diagonal machinery of *Glen Sannox*. These were one of the most powerful sets of paddle steamer machinery anywhere in Britain.

Glen Sannox on the slipway at Blackwood & Gordon, Port Glasgow, for winter refit.

After the pooling arrangement with the CSP on the Arran service in 1908, each company took the Arran service in alternate years. In 1910 *Glen Sannox*, along with *Atalanta*, was laid up in the West Harbour at Greenock, and in 1912 was placed on the run to Arran via the Kyles. She is seen here in Rothesay Bay in 1922 in a George Stromier photo.

Glen Sannox on an unusual call, or faked photograph, at Ormidale. In 1915 she was requisitioned and sent down to Southampton for trooping service to France. It is believed she made only one such trip and that the weather proved too much for her light build. She was sent back to the Clyde after only a month and spent the remainder of the war back on the Ardrossan to Arran service.

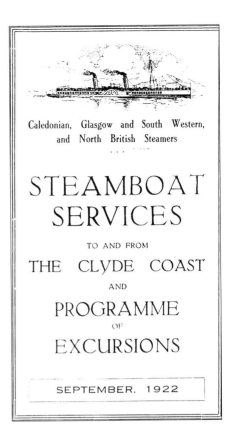

Caledonian, Glasgow and South Western, and North British Steamers

. . .

STEAMBOAT SERVICES

TO AND FROM

THE CLYDE COAST

AND

PROGRAMME

OF

EXCURSIONS

SEPTEMBER, 1922

Glen Sannox featured on the cover of the combined GSWR, CSP and NB timetable for September 1922.

In 1923, now under LMS ownership, the GSWR steamers sailed with tricolour funnels and a grey hull. For the 1924 season black had replaced grey as the hull colour, and *Glen Sannox* is seen here approaching Brodick in that year. Some of the steamers had a deep red band on the funnel in 1923, and some a narrower band. All had a narrow red band in 1924.

Glen Sannox approaching Lamlash in 1924, which was to prove her final season. Note the LMS flag at the top of the mast also, in the background, a warship of the Channel Fleet, with a small naval launch in the foreground.

From September 1924 until May 1925 *Glen Sannox* lay in the Albert Harbour, Greenock, as seen here. A new boiler was required and it was deemed more cost-effective to built a turbine replacement. On 22 May 1925 she was towed to the shipbreakers at Port Glasgow and broken up after the next few months.

Mercury was a sister of *Neptune*, coming from the same builders and engine-makers. She entered service at the end of May and spent most of her career on the Kyles of Bute service.

Mercury in the Kyles of Bute.

POPULAR DAILY EXCURSION.

To THE ISLAND of ARRAN,

BY THE SALOON STEAMER

"MERCURY" or "JUPITER"

Train Leaves St. Enoch at 8-45 a.m.

STEAMER leaves Princes Pier, Greenock, 9-45 a.m., Kirn 10-10, Dunoon 10-15, Innellan 10-30, Craigmore 10-50, Rothesay 11-0 a.m., thence through the Kyles of Bute, calling at Tighnabruaich at 11-40 a.m., passing Ardlamont Point, Inchmarnock, and thence direct to Arran, calling at Corrie, Brodick, Lamlash, King's Cross, and arrive at Whiting Bay about 1-40 p.m.

Returning from Whiting Bay at 2-0,* Lamlash 2-20,* Brodick 2-45,* and Corrie at 3-5* p.m., thence via Garrochhead (south end of Bute) and Mount Stuart (the residence of the Marquis of Bute) to Rothesay, Innellan, Dunoon, and Kirn, arriving back in Greenock about 5-20 p.m Train in connection for Glasgow at 5-30 p.m.

* Steamer returns from all Ports 45 minutes later on Saturdays. Train from Princes Pier 6-10 p.m.

Passengers for Kyles of Bute change at Rothesay and join G. & S.-W. Steamer at 4-0 and 5-35 p.m. except Sats., and on Sats. at 7-45 p.m.

Return Fares.

	1st Class. and Saloon.	3rd Class and Saloon.	3rd Class and Steerage.
From Glasgow or Paisley to Arran and Back,	4s. 9d.	3s. 6d.	3s. 0d.
		Saloon.	Fore Saloon.
„ Greenock,		3s. 6d.	2s. 6d.
„ Dunoon and Innellan,		3s. 0d.	2s. 0d.
„ Rothesay,		2s. 6d.	1s. 6d.
„ Kyles of Bute,		2s. 6d.	1s. 6d.

SPECIAL AFTERNOON SAIL,

ARRAN to ROTHESAY,

TUESDAYS, 4th and 18th AUGUST.

From Whiting Bay at 2-0; King's Cross 1-30; Lamlash 2-20; Brodick 2-45; Corrie 3-5 p.m. Arriving at Rothesay at 4-5 p.m., and returning at 5-40 p.m., via Kyles of Bute.

RETURN FARE, 1s. 6d. **Available Day of Issue only.**

For Coach Tour in Bute, see page 11.
For Circular Tour to Island of Arran, via Ardrossan, see page 12.
For Coach Tour in Arran, via Lochranza, see page 11.
For Circular Coach and Steamer Tour between Greenock, Rothesay and Largs, see page 11.

A page from the August 1896 timetable, showing the Arran via the Kyles cruise offered by *Mercury* or *Jupiter*.

Mercury approaching Rothesay with Craigmore Pier in the background. St John's church spire on the extreme right is the only one still standing, the other two having been demolished.

Mercury was requisitioned as a minesweeper in the First World War, and was based at Harwich. She had both her bow and stern blown off in separate incidents, but was repaired on each occasion.

Mercury arriving at Dunoon in 1923 with grey hull and 'tartan lum'. *(A. Ernest Glen collection)*

Mercury in 1924 in the East Kyle, now with a black hull and now with a narrow red band on the funnel.

Mercury arriving at Dunoon. Note the small canvas dodger forward on the promenade deck. This was for a look out required by regulations for steamers with the bridge aft of the funnel.

THE PIER, INNELLAN.

Mercury at Innellan in a postcard view in LMS colours.

Mercury at Wemyss Bay. She sailed on railway-connected runs from there, Greenock and Gourock, until December 1933 when she was sold for scrapping at Barrow.

Minerva was built in 1893 by J&G Thomson, entering service on 1 June of that year. She mainly served on routes from Princes Pier, although she was more strongly built than the other steamers and was suited for all-the-year-round service.

Minerva racing *Meg Merrilies*. *(A. Ernest Glen collection)*

Minerva tendering to the Cunard Liner *Lusitania*, whilst the latter was on trials in 1907. *Minerva* was purchased by the Admiralty in 1915, and was based at Malta and in the eastern Mediterranean as an Admiralty Patrol Paddler. She served as a minesweeper from 1919 to 1920 and was paid off at Constantinople in June of that year. It has been stated that she was sold to Turkish owners, and she continued to appear in Lloyds Register under anonymous Turkish ownership until 1928, but those researching Turkish steamers have been unable to find any trace of her.

⊷ EXCURSION ⊷

To ARROCHAR (Loch Long)

For LOCH LOMOND.

By Saloon Steamers "MINERVA" or "GLEN ROSA."

TRAIN FROM ST. ENOCH AT 10·5 A.M. (except Saturdays).

(Saturday Afternoon Sail, see page 14.)

Steamer leaves Greenock (Old Pier) at 10·30 a.m.; Princes Pier at 11·0; Rothesay at 9·45; Craigmore, 9·50; Innellan, 10·10; Dunoon, 10·25; Kirn, 10·30; Hunter's Quay, 10·35; Kilcreggan, 11·10; Blairmore, 11·20 a.m. Arriving at Arrochar about 12·20 p.m.

Steamer returns Daily, except Saturdays, at 2·45 p.m. Train to Paisley and Glasgow, 4·15 p.m.

Passengers are thereby afforded ample time to walk or drive to and from Loch Lomond, which is little over a mile distant from Arrochar Pier—Coach Fare, 6d. each way—where they join Steamer and sail down Loch Lomond to Balloch. Train to Glasgow and Greenock.

RETURN FARES:

From GREENOCK, ROTHESAY, DUNOON, INNELLAN, or KILCREGGAN, ... Saloon, **2s.**; Fore Saloon, **1s. 6d.**

„ BLAIRMORE, ... „ **1s. 6d.**; „ **1s. 6d.**

FARES for CIRCULAR TOUR from GREENOCK to ARROCHAR and LOCH LOMOND, returning via BALLOCH and GLASGOW:

First Class and Steamer, **5s.**; Third Class and Steamer, **3s. 11d.**

⊷ EXCURSION ⊷

To LARGS, MILLPORT, and KILCHATTAN BAY.

Train leaves St. Enoch at 8·45 a.m.

Steamer from Princes Pier at 9·45 a.m., Kirn 10·10, Dunoon 10·15, Innellan 10·30 a.m., thence to Rothesay, where Passengers change into G. & S.·W. Steamer, leaving there at 11·15 a.m. for

Largs, Millport, and Kilchattan Bay.

Returning from Kilchattan Bay at 2·30 p.m. except Sats. (4·5 p.m. Sats. only), Millport 3·40 daily, Largs 4·5 p.m. except Sats., and change at Rothesay into G. & S.·W. Steamer leaving at (5·0 and 6·15 p.m. Sats. only) 6·50 p.m. daily, and 3·0 p.m. Saturdays for Greenock, calling at Innellan, Dunoon, and Kirn.

RETURN FARES:

From GREENOCK, ... Saloon, **1s. 6d.**; Fore Saloon, **1s.**

„ KIRN, DUNOON, .. „ **1s. 6d.**; „ **1s.**

„ INNELLAN, ... „ **1s.**; „ **1s.**

Coach Tour, see page 14.

The August 1896 timetable for the trip to Arrochar, offered by *Minerva* or *Glen Rosa*.

Glen Rosa was a sister of *Minerva* and was designed for the winter Arran service, hence the deviation from the standard Roman deity nomenclature. She entered service about a month after her sister, and spent her first three seasons on the Ayr excursion roster. Her summer route from around 1912 was from Fairlie to Rothesay via Millport and Kilchattan Bay.

Glen Rosa approaching Greenock Custom House Quay. In spite of the proximity of Princes Pier some GSWR sailings called at both piers.

Glen Rosa lying at Arrochar in 1899 with *Lady Rowena* and *Ivanhoe* in an F.S. Easton photo.

Glen Rosa at Kirn Pier. She saw war service as the minesweeper HMS *Glencross* from May 1917 until April 1919.

Glen Rosa leaving Largs in her 1924 condition.

Glen Rosa in 1925 approaching Rothesay. After the 1925 season she was reboilered and her bridge placed forward of the funnel. 1925 was the only year in which she appeared in this condition.

A well-filled *Glen Rosa* in Rothesay Bay, post-1925. The LMS flag can be clearly seen here, and there is a white disc where the GSWR crest has been removed from the paddle box.

A stern view of *Glen Rosa* leaving Innellan, post-1925. After the 1936 season she was used on special excursions and 'spare' duties. In 1938 she was transferred to CSP ownership, and was laid up in the following year, being sold for breaking up at Dalmuir in August 1939.

Jupiter was a larger steamer than the three previous steamers built by J&G Thomson in 1896. She was plated right up to the bow like *Glen Sannox*, but only had one funnel and was 30ft shorter.

Jupiter was placed on the Arran via the Kyles service, replacing *Neptune* there in competition with *Ivanhoe*. After the cooperation agreement in 1908 she sailed on that service in 1910 and 1914.

The Arran via the Kyles service involved a ferry call at Corrie, passengers being ferried ashore from *Jupiter* by a fleet of rowing boats. (*A. Ernest Glen collection*)

Jupiter at Brodick, with *Glen Sannox* having just left the pier.

There was a further ferry call at Kings Cross, between Lamlash and Whiting Bay. *Jupiter* is here on her homeward journey which was made via Garroch Head.

Jupiter served as the minesweeper *Jupiter II* during the First World War and, after her return to service in 1920, operated on longer distance excursions from Greenock. She ran Round the Lochs on Mondays and Wednesdays, to Ayr on Tuesdays and Thursdays, and on an afternoon cruise to the Kyles of Bute on Saturdays. On some Sunday afternoons she offered a cruise round Bute. She is seen here at Rothesay in June 1923. (*A. Ernest Glen collection*)

SPECIAL EVENING CRUISES

(Weather favourable)

By Saloon Steamer "JUPITER" or "MERCURY."

FRIDAY, 7th AUGUST,	FRIDAY, 14th AUGUST,
SKIPNESS & ROUND SKATE ISLAND (Lochfyne).	**ROUND THE ISLAND OF BUTE**

From Craigmore at 5-30 p.m., Rothesay 3-35, Port-Bannatyne 5-45;
arriving back about 9-30 p.m.

Return Fare, One Shilling.

EVENING CRUISES
By Saloon Steamer, "JUPITER" OR "MERCURY."

From Craigmore at 6-45, Rothesay 7-0, Port-Bannatyne 7-10 p.m.

5th and 18th AUGUST,	
To LOCHRANZA Calling at Innellan at 7-30 and Dunoon at 7-45 p.m. on 7th, 14th, and 19th Aug.	**7th, 14th, & 19th AUG.,** **To LOCHGOIL.**
12th AUGUST, **To BRODICK BAY.**	**17th AUGUST,** **ROUND BUTE.**

Return Fare, One Shilling.

For full particulars of Evening Excursions, see Posters at various Coast Piers.

ON BOARD OF ALL THE STEAMERS
BREAKFASTS, LUNCHEONS, DINNERS, and TEAS
Are Served on the Shortest Notice, and at Moderate Charges

Coupons for either Breakfast, Luncheon, or Tea transferable, and available on board any of the Company's Steamers, are also sold in lots of 12 at **18/-.** The Coupons can be used for Dinner on payment of **1/-** extra.

RATES FOR STEAMBOAT SEASON TICKETS.

	One Month	Two Months	Three Months
Greenock (Lynedoch Street) to Kilmun and Rothesay Section only, ...	15/	25/	35/
,, and Lochgoilhead Section only, ...	17/6	32/6	45/
,, and Kyles of Bute ,, ...	17/6	32/6	45/
,, and Arran Section, ...	20/	37/6	50/
Ardrossan and Arran, ...	17/6	32/6	45/
All Sections and all Excursions by Coy.'s Steamers, ...	22/	41/	56/6

Deposit, 2/6 each.

These Season Tickets are not Transferable and are only valid for the Sections printed thereon. Young Persons under 14 and under 18 years of age are charged One-Third and One-Half the Adult Rates respectively.

A Discount will be allowed when more than one Adult Ticket is taken out by same family.

PLEASURE PARTIES, PIC-NICS, AND SABBATH SCHOOL EXCURSIONS

Will be conveyed by Special or Ordinary Steamers to and from any of the places on the Coast at **Reduced Fares,** on application being made to Captain ALEX. WILLIAMSON, Marine Superintendent, Princes Pier, Greenock, not later than two clear days prior to the date on which such parties intend to travel.

A programme of evening cruises was offered by *Jupiter* or *Mercury* as seen in this extract from the August 1896 timetable.

Jupiter at Rothesay Pier in 1924 colours, with a black hull and thinner red band on the funnel than in 1923.

An almost empty *Jupiter* approaching Hunter's Quay in post-1924 colours.

A well-filled *Jupiter* departing from Dunoon in LMS colours.

After the advent of the new *Caledonia* and *Mercury* in 1934, *Jupiter* was relegated to the Wemyss Bay and Largs to Millport run. She was withdrawn after the 1935 season and sold in December of that year for scrapping at Barrow-in-Furness.

THE ROUND OF THE LOCHS AND THE FIRTH OF CLYDE

By Steamer "JUPITER" or other Steamer
(Weather favourable)

which includes the round of the Islands of Bute and Cumbrae, Kyles of Bute, Loch Ridden, Loch Striven, Loch Goil, and Loch Long—is generally conceded to be the most popular excursion on the Clyde. It embraces in one day a wide range and variety of scenery which can only be equalled by spending several days on board the various Excursion Steamers.

MONDAYS and WEDNESDAYS only. Commences 11th JUNE
(Monday, 16th July, and Wednesday, 1st August, excepted.)

STATIONS.		*Via* Greenock.	*Via* Gourock.	*Via* Wemyss Bay.
		a.m.	a.m.	a.m.
Glasgow (St. Enoch)	Train leaves	7 30	..	..
Glasgow (Central)	,,	..	8 0	8 55
Paisley (Gilmour Street)	,,	7 45	8 13	9 7
Greenock (Central)	,,	..	8 47	..
Greenock (West)	,,	..	8 51	..
Greenock (Princes Pier)	Steamer leaves	8 45	...	..
Gourock	,,	..	9 5	..
Dunoon	,,	9 20		..
Innellan	,,	9 37		..
Wemyss Bay	,,	..		9 55
Craigmore	,,		10 20	
Rothesay	,,		10 30	
Largs	,,		11 5	
Millport (Keppel)	,,		11 23	
Millport (Old Pier)	,,		11 30	

THENCE ROUND THE LOCHS.

			p.m.	
†Millport (Old Pier)	Steamer arrives		6 15	
†Millport (Keppel)	,,		6 8	
†Largs	,,		5 50	
Wemyss Bay	,,		5 20	
Craigmore	,,		5 45	
Rothesay	,,		5 50	
‡Innellan	,,		5 30	
Dunoon	,,		5 0	
‡Gourock	,,		5 50	
‡Greenock (Princes Pier)	,,		6 5	

		Via Wemyss Bay	*Via* Gourock	*Via* Greenock (Prin. Pr.)
Greenock (West)	Train arrives	..	6 8	..
Greenock (Central)	,,	..	6 11	..
Paisley (Gilmour Street)	,,	6 45	6 37	6c41
Glasgow (Central)	,,	7 4	6 56	..
Glasgow (St. Enoch)	,,	..	..	6 58

† Passengers returning to Largs and Millport change at Wemyss Bay.
‡ Passengers returning to Innellan, Gourock, and Greenock change at Dunoon. Exchange Tickets to be had at Ticket Office. c Canal Station.

The timetable for *Jupiter's* Round of the Lochs and Firth of Clyde cruise in summer 1928.

Juno was built in 1898 by the Clydebank Engineering & Shipbuilding Co. Ltd, which was the new name of the yard of J&G Thomson in 1897. She had been ordered for the Planet Steamers of Mrs C Black who operated *Jupiter*, originally *Lord of the Isles* of 1877 from the Inveraray route, on cruises from London to Southend and Margate. They went into liquidation and *Juno* was offered, part-built, to the GSWR. (*A. Ernest Glen collection*).

A GSWR official card of *Juno*.

Juno offered a wide variety of excursions from Ayr, from where she is seen leaving here.

Many of these excursions were also offered from Troon.

Juno departing astern from Troon in a postcard view, with the paddle tug *Troon* half-hidden by the breakwater on the right.

Juno also made made occasional calls at Girvan at high tide.

PLEASURE SAILING

- FROM -

AYR, TROON, ARDROSSAN, LARGS, &c.,

By Saloon Steamer "JUNO" or other Steamer.

NOTE.—The Company reserve the right to alter or cancel any Excursion or Evening Cruise if necessary.

SATURDAYS, 17th and 24th JULY.

17th.

Forenoon—TO ARRAN

(Brodick, Lamlash, and Whiting Bay).

OUTWARD.	a.m.	INWARD.	p.m.
Ayr,	dep. 11 0	Whiting Bay,	dep. 2 30
Troon,	,, 11 30	Lamlash,	,, 2 50
Brodick,	arr. abt. 12 30p	Brodick,	,, 3 15
Lamlash,	,, 12 55	Ayr,	arr. abt. 4 30
Whiting Bay,	,, 1 15	Troon,	,, 5 30

Return Fares—Cabin, 2/; Steerage, 1/6.

NOTE.—Passengers will have about two and a half hours ashore at Brodick, one hour and a half at Lamlash, and one hour and fifteen minutes at Whiting Bay.

EVENING CRUISE TO KILCHATTAN BAY,

From AYR and TROON.

OUTWARD.	p.m.	INWARD.	p.m.
Ayr,	dep. 5 0	Kilchattan Bay,	dep. 8 0
Troon,	,, 5 30	Troon,	arr. abt. 9 15
Kilchattan Bay,	arr. abt. 6 45	Ayr,	,, 9 45

Return Fare—1/.

24th.

Forenoon—Round LITTLE CUMBRAE,

From AYR and TROON.

OUTWARD.	a.m.	INWARD.	p.m.
Ayr,	dep. 10 45	Troon,	arr. abt. 1 30
Troon,	,, 11 15	Ayr,	,, 2 0
Thence Round Little Cumbrae.		Return Fare, 1/6.	

Afternoon—To Girvan and Round Ailsa Craig,

From TROON and AYR.

OUTWARD.	p.m.	INWARD.	p.m.
Troon,	dep. 1 30	Girvan,	dep. 5 15
Ayr,	,, 2 30	Ayr,	arr. abt. 6 30
Girvan,	arr. abt. 3 45	Troon,	,, 7 30
Thence Round Ailsa Craig, arriving back at Girvan about 5.5 p.m.		Return Fare— Troon or Ayr to Girvan and Round Ailsa Craig, 1/6.	

NOTE.—Passengers landing at Girvan at 3.45 p.m. will have about one hour and twenty minutes ashore.

EVENING CRUISE to BRODICK BAY.

From Ayr at 7.0 p.m., arriving back at Ayr about 10.0 p.m.

Return Fare—1/.

MONDAY, 19th JULY.

To STRANRAER

(LOCH RYAN),

From ARDROSSAN, TROON, and AYR.

OUTWARD.	a.m.	INWARD.	p.m.
Ardrossan,	dep. 9 35	Stranraer,	dep. 3 30
Troon,	,, 10 10	Ayr,	arr. abt. 6 0
Ayr,	,, 11 0	Troon,	dep. 6 20
Stranraer,	arr. abt. 1 30p	Ardrossan,	arr. abt. 6 50
			,, 7 30

RETURN FARES.	Cab.	Stg.
Ardrossan, Troon, or Ayr to Stranraer,	3/6	2/6

TUESDAY, 20th JULY.

To LOCHGOILHEAD.

OUTWARD.	a.m.	INWARD.	p.m.
Ayr,	dep. 10 0	Lochgoilhead,	dep. 2 50
Troon,	,, 10 30	Largs,	,, 4 20
Ardrossan,	,, 11 5	Ardrossan,	arr. abt. 5 15
Largs,	,, 12. 0n	Troon,	,, 5 50
Lochgoilhead,	arr. abt. 1 30p	Ayr,	,, 6 30

Passengers have time to drive from Lochgoilhead through part of Glasgow's New Estate (Ardgoil) and back.
RETURN COACH FARE, 1/.

RETURN FARES.	Cab.	Stg.
Ayr or Troon to Lochgoilhead,	3/6	2/6
Ardrossan to Lochgoilhead,	3/	2/
Ayr or Troon to Largs,	2/6	2/
Largs to Lochgoilhead,	2/6	2/

WEDNESDAY, 21st JULY—ROTHESAY FAIR (First Day).

SPECIAL DAY EXCURSIONS TO ROTHESAY.

From AYR.

OUTWARD.	a.m.	INWARD.	p.m.
Ayr,	dep. 10 0	Rothesay,	dep. 2 20
Largs,	,, 11 30	Largs,	,, 2 50
Rothesay,	arr. abt. 12 0n	Ayr,	arr. abt. 4 20

RETURN FARES.	Cab.	Stg.
Ayr to Largs or Rothesay,	2/6	2/
Largs to Rothesay,	1/	2/

From TROON and ARDROSSAN.

OUTWARD.	a.m.	INWARD.	p.m.
Troon,	dep. 10 30	Rothesay,	dep. 2 45
Ardrossan,	,, 11 5	Largs,	arr. abt. 3 15
Largs,	,, 12 0n	Ardrossan,	,, 4 10
Rothesay,	,, 12 30p	Troon,	,, 4 55

RETURN FARES.	Cab.	Stg.
Troon to Largs or Rothesay,	2/6	2/
Ardrossan to Largs,	1/6	2/
Ardrossan to Rothesay,	2/	1/6

NOTE.—Tickets are not available on Evening Cruise Return Journey from Rothesay.

FOR LIST OF EVENING CRUISES SEE OTHER SIDE.

A copy of a handbill for sailings by *Juno* from 17 to 24 July, probably in 1909.

The two-cylinder compound engines of *Juno*.

Juno at the short-lived pier at Portencross, south of Hunterston. The pier was built in 1912, but sailings ceased on the outbreak of war in 1914. It was used a destination for both scheduled and mystery cruises. The pier was used in a special sailing by *Waverley* in 1995 after a gap of eighty-one years since it was last used.

Juno approaching Brodick.

Juno was requisitioned in January 1915. She served in the First World War as the minesweeper HMS *Junior*, and is seen here with another, unidentified, paddle minesweeper and a naval steam trawler. She saw service initially in the Firth of Clyde minesweeping between Ardrossan and Troon, and later in the Firth of Forth, based at Granton. She returned to Clyde service in 1919 on services from Princes Pier to Rothesay. She is seen here with P.&A. Campbell's *Glen Usk* in the background.

Juno returned to the Ayr excursion service in 1920, and is seen here at Rothesay in 1923.

Juno with the turbine *Glen Sannox* of 1925 in Ayr harbour on a Sunday in summer 1925. She is at Compass Pier, now used by *Waverley*. (*CRSC archive*)

Juno in Rothesay Bay in LMS post-1924 colours.

Juno approaching Rothesay. She served from Ayr until withdrawn after the 1931 season, and was sold in spring 1932 for breaking up at Alloa.

LONDON MIDLAND AND SCOTTISH RAILWAY

DAILY SAILINGS

By STEAMER

"JUNO"

FROM

AYR, TROON, ARDROSSAN, GIRVAN
MILLPORT
LARGS and ARRAN PIERS

SEASON 1926

The cover of *Juno's* excursion brochure for 1926.

PLEASURE SAILINGS

FROM GIRVAN
(WEATHER FAVOURABLE)

By Steamer "JUNO"
JULY, 1930.

MONDAY, 7th JULY—Leave Girvan Harbour at 8.20 a.m.

ROTHESAY and ORMIDALE
(LOCH RIDDEN)

Calling at Ayr, Troon, Ardrossan, Millport (Keppel) and Largs.
Allowing about 2¼ hours ashore at Rothesay and 1¼ hours at Ormidale
Arriving back at Girvan at 8 p.m.

SATURDAY, 19th JULY—Leave Girvan Harbour at 5.15 p.m.

ROUND AILSA CRAIG
Arriving back at Girvan at 6.45 p.m.

TUESDAY, 22nd JULY—Leave Girvan Harbour at 8.20 a.m.

DUNOON

Calling at Ayr, Troon, Millport (Keppel) and Largs.
Allowing about 2 hours on shore at Dunoon.
Arriving back at Girvan at 8 p.m.

SATURDAY, 26th JULY—Leave Girvan Harbour at 11.30 a.m.

ROUND AILSA CRAIG
Arriving back at Girvan at 1 p.m.

RETURN FARES:

To ROTHESAY or DUNOON,	... ...	Cabin, 5/6.	Steerage, 4/-
" ORMIDALE, ...	... ...	" 6/-	" 4/6
" ROUND AILSA CRAIG,	... ...	" 1/6	—

1930   J. H. FOLLOWS, Vice-President.

AYRSHIRE POST, LTD., AYR.

Reproduced from a Sailing Bill in the Club's Collection

Sailings from Girvan recommenced in 1926. Above is a handbill of 1930 sailings.

1902 saw the building of the final GSWR paddler, *Mars*, by the usual yard which had by now been taken over by the Sheffield engineering firm of John Brown. She was smaller version of *Jupiter*, with the promenade deck extended to the bow.

A stern view of *Mars* heading away from Princes Pier.

A smoky *Mars* in mid-firth. Note the exceptionally small paddle boxes.

Mars at Greenock's Princes Pier in as postcard view.

Glasgow & South-Western Railway Steamers.

PAISLEY : FAIR : SATURDAY,
10TH AUGUST.

Special Excursions

AS UNDER

By Saloon Steamer "MARS."

(WEATHER FAVOURABLE)

To ROTHESAY
AND KYLES OF BUTE
(LOCH RIDDEN.)

From ARDROSSAN (Winton Pier) 9.30 a.m., arriving at ROTHESAY about 11 o'clock, thence Cruise through KYLES OF BUTE to LOCH RIDDEN; Returning from ROTHESAY at 1 p.m., arriving back at ARDROSSAN about 2.30 p.m.

RETURN FARES—

To Rothesay, - Cabin, 2s; Steerage, 1s 6d.

„ Kyles of Bute, - 2s 6d.

NEW CUNARD STEAMER,

"LUSITANIA"

The Largest and Fastest Vessel Afloat.

SPECIAL AFTERNOON CRUISE round the Ship lying off Greenock,

From ARDROSSAN (Winton Pier) - 2.30 p.m.

and arriving back about 6.30 p.m.

Return Fare, = Two Shillings.

For Train connections see Time Tables.

Marine Superintendent's Office, } A 230   DAVID COOPER, General Manager.
Greenock, August, 1907.

CHRISTIE, PRINTER, ARDROSSAN.

A handbill for sailings by *Mars* from Ardrossan on Paisley Fair Saturday 10 August 1907, including an afternoon cruise to sail round the *Lusitania*, which would then be on her trials

Mars leaving Greenock Princes Pier. She was called up for minesweeping duties on 22 September 1916 as HMS *Marsa*, and was run down by a destroyer during the night of 18 November 1918 off Harwich. She settled on a sandbank, but broke in two during salvage attempts.

In 1902 the GSWR took over Troon harbour from the Duke of Portland. In the same year a new paddle tug, *Troon*, was built for the port by Rennoldson of South Shields. She had two-cylinder side-lever engines and remained in service until 1930 when she was sold to Middlesbrough. In 1934 she was again sold and in 1948 was scrapped. She is seen here in September 1922 and behind her is the Argentine coastal passenger liner *José Menendez*, which was completed that year at the Ailsa yard. (*A. Ernest Glen collection*)

In 1904 the GSWR purchased a steamer named *Britannia* from Capt. John Williamson, who had just purchased her from the Hastings, St-Leonards-on-Sea and Eastbourne Steamboat Co. Ltd. She had been built in 1897 by Russell & Co. with machinery by Rankin and Blackmore for John Williamson as *Kylemore* but sold to the south of England company whilst on the stocks. She was renamed *Vulcan* by the GSWR and served the Fairlie to Millport run, but after the cooperation agreement with the CSP in 1908 was sold back to Capt. Williamson, who named her *Kylemore* again. She served him and his successors, mainly on the Rothesay to Glasgow service, until taken up for war service in 1939 and was sunk off Harwich in 1940. She is seen here arriving at Kilchattan Bay.

In autumn 1905 John Brown had a set of experimental turbines in stock, built as a trial model for those fitted in Cunard's *Campania*. These were offered to the GSWR and fitted in their only turbine steamer, the triple screw *Atalanta*. She entered service in June of that year, offering in the first week of her career, excursions from Ayr. She is seen here on trials. During her first season she offered cruises on the whole firth, even as far as Stranraer.

Atalanta was smaller and slower than the Denny-built turbines but could still attract the crowds. Her bridge was placed forward of the funnel, and she was the first GSWR steamer to be designed as such.

Atalanta served on a variety of excursions in her pre-1914 career, including Greenock to Ayr in 1906, Greenock to Stranraer in 1907 and Arrochar in 1908. She was spare steamer on the Arran run and is seen here in a postcard view at Whiting Bay. In 1910 she was laid up for the summer.

On 8 May 1913 *Atalanta* ran aground after leaving Whiting Bay. Sand and weed had been sucked into the circulating pumps causing the engines to stop. There were only twelve passengers on board and they were landed by the ship's boats. *Atalanta* was towed off on 11 May and was out of service until 15 July.

Atalanta served as a troop transport on the English Channel from February to December 1915 and as the minesweeper HMS *Atalanta II*, as seen here, until spring 1919, mainly out of Harwich. The dropesa gear on her stern can be seen here. (*A. Ernest Glen collection*)

Atalanta returned to Clyde service on 27 June 1919 and served as secondary Arran steamer in the post-war years. She is seen here in 1923 colours. *(A. Ernest Glen collection)*

Atalanta off Dunoon in her 1924 colour scheme.

Atalanta in Rothesay Bay in 1924, still with the 'tartan lum'.

Atalanta arriving at Whiting Bay in the post-1924 LMS livery. She was reboilered in 1930.

Daily Excursions

By Turbine Steamers "Glen Sannox" and "Atalanta"

Via Ardrossan

To the ISLAND OF ARRAN

For "GLEN SANNOX."—Train leaves Glasgow (St. Enoch) 9-5 a.m., Paisley (Gilmour Street) 9-20 a.m.

For "ATALANTA."—Train leaves Glasgow (Central) a8-30 a.m. (commences 29th June).

"Glen Sannox" leaves Ardrossan (Winton Pier) at 10-10 a.m. for Brodick, Lamlash and Whiting Bay.

"Atalanta" (commencing 29th June) leaves Ardrossan (Montgomerie Pier) at 9-35 a.m. for Whiting Bay, Lamlash and Brodick.

Passengers return, except Saturdays, by "Glen Sannox" from Whiting Bay at 2-55 p.m., Lamlash 3-15 p.m., Brodick 3-40 p.m., and by "Atalanta" (commencing 29th June) from Whiting Bay 4-15 p.m., Lamlash 4-40 p.m., Brodick 5-10 p.m.

a From 13th to 31st August Passengers leave Glasgow (Central) at 8-0 a.m. (Saturdays excepted).

For Saturday Return Sailings see page 26.

On 30th and 31st July and 30th and 31st August an Altered Service will be in operation. See pages 25 and 26.

RETURN FARES.

From Glasgow or Paisley	1st & Cabin, 10/6 ;	3rd & Cabin, 7/-
„ Ardrossan ..	Cabin, 3/6 ;	Steerage 2/7½

Afternoon Excursions

By Turbine Steamers "Glen Sannox" and "Atalanta"
Via Ardrossan

To the ISLAND OF ARRAN

On Saturdays Trains leave Glasgow (Central) at 12-30 p.m. (commencing 30th June), Glasgow (St. Enoch) 1-55 p.m.

Except Saturdays, Train leaves Glasgow (St. Enoch) at 12-20 p.m. (commencing 29th June). On 2nd July and 1st August leaves at 1-15 p.m.

Returning on Saturdays from Whiting Bay 4-45 p.m., Lamlash 5-5 p.m., Brodick 5-30 p.m., and except Saturdays (commencing 29th June) from Whiting Bay 4-15 p.m., Lamlash 4-40 p.m., Brodick 5-10 p.m.

On 30th and 31st July and 30th and 31st August an Altered Service will be in operation. See pages 25 and 26.

RETURN FARES.

From Glasgow and Paisley ..	1st & Cabin, 7/6 ;	3rd & Cabin, 5/6
„ Ardrossan	Cabin, 2/6 ;	Steerage, 1/9

In 1928 *Atalanta* was on the Ardrossan (Montgomerie Pier) to Brodick service as detailed in the enclosed page from the 1928 summer timetable.

Replaced by *Duchess of Hamilton* in the 1931 season, *Atalanta* went onto a variety of up-firth services. From spring 1936 to March 1937 she maintained the Wemyss Bay and Fairlie to Millport services.

On 25 June 1936 *Atalanta* ran aground in Millport Bay in fog whilst arriving from Kilchattan Bay. The ship's boats evacuated the twelve passengers and she was refloated on the next tide.

In March 1937 *Atalanta* was sold to the Blackpool Steam Navigation Co. for excursions from Blackpool and Morecambe, including day trips to Llandudno, which she carried out until outbreak of war. In 1937 she also provided a service from Fleetwood to Barrow-in-Furness connecting with the LMS Lake District day excursions. A solid bridge front of varnished wood was fitted in that year.

Atalanta served as a boom and net inspection vessel and netlayer during the Second World War. She lay out of use at Methil, seen above, after the war until sold in October 1946 for breaking up at Ghent.

LOCHRANZA – PIRNMILL — CARRADALE

AND

CAMPBELTOWN

FOR

BLACKWATERFOOT and MACHRIHANISH

BY

"DALRIADA" and "DAVAAR"

—— WITH SPECIAL SAILINGS ——
DURING GLASGOW FAIR HOLIDAYS

AND

DAY AND AFTERNOON EXCURSIONS

—— 1st JUNE to 31st AUGUST, 1938 ——

For further particulars apply to

CLYDE & CAMPBELTOWN SHIPPING COMPANY, LTD.

171/175 CLYDE STREET, and BRIDGE WHARF, GLASGOW
(Telephone No. : 973 Central)

CUSTOM HOUSE QUAY, GREENOCK, or CAMPBELTOWN
(Telephone No. 834)   (Telephone No. 2)

A 1938 advertisement for the Clyde and Campbeltown Shipping Co. Ltd's service to Campbeltown.

Two
Campbeltown and Glasgow Steamers

Gael was built in 1867 by Robertson & Co. of Greenock, with two-cylinder simple oscillating engines by Rankin & Blackmore. She was originally flush-decked as seen here and operated day trips to Lochranza, Carradale and Campbeltown from Greenock. She is seen here off Greenock.

THE KILBRANNAN ROUTE.

GLASGOW & CAMPBELTOWN,

CALLING AT

GREENOCK, LOCHRANZA, PIRNMILL (ARRAN), AND CARRADALE,

OCT.,
1882.

The

Powerful

OCT.,
1882.

And

Commodious

Steamers

GAEL, KINLOCH, OR KINTYRE,

With Goods and Passengers will sail (unless prevented by any unforeseen occurrence) between CAMPBELTOWN, GREENOCK, and GLASGOW, with liberty in the option of the Captains to go through the KYLES OF BUTE, and to call at WEMYSS BAY, BOWLING, RENFREW, and other intermediate ports.

From Campbeltown	From Glasgow
Every	Every
TUESDAY,	TUESDAY,
WEDNESDAY,	WEDNESDAY,
THURSDAY,	THURSDAY,
AND *SATURDAY,	AND SATURDAY,
At EIGHT O'CLOCK MORNING,	AND FRIDAY, THE 6TH,
	At EIGHT O'CLOCK MORNING,
AND FRIDAY, THE 6TH, AT 7 A.M.	TRAINS TO GREENOCK :—
*ON SATURDAY, THE 7TH AT 7 A.M.	CENTRAL, ... AT 10.0 A.M.
	ST. ENOCH, ... AT 10.5 A.M.

FARES :—Campbeltown or Carradale to Glasgow, Cabin, 5s; Steerage, 2s 6d. Lochranza to Glasgow, Cabin, 4s : Steerage, 2s; or *Vice Versa.*

Goods and Cattle must be on the Quay ONE HOUR before the time of Sailing, and two days' notice given to the Manager of all Live Stock for Shipment.

Horses, Cattle, and all Live Stock, are shipped, carried, and landed at their owners' risk and responsibility ; and must be accompanied by the owner or his servant.

Passengers are requested to take charge of their own luggage, as the Company is not responsible in any way for its safety Cabin Passengers allowed 84 lbs. personal luggage ; Steerage Passengers 56 lbs.

The Company will not be responsible for empty packages returned, unless the same are booked and paid for ; otherwise these returns are entirely at the risk of the parties sending them. Nor for any article whatever, unless booked and signed for before being shipped.

Freight on Goods per Steamer is payable on delivery.

Freight on Goods to the Coast must be paid before shipment, and Goods forwarded on condition that they are at shippers' risk.

Apply to R. M. DUNLOP, 22 Anderston Quay, Glasgow ; JOHN MACMILLAN, India Place No. 1, Open Shore, Greenock ; or here to

CAMPBELTOWN, 20th Sept., 1882.   JOHN MURRAY, MANAGER.

An October 1882 advertisement for sailings to Campbeltown by *Gael*, *Kintyre*, and *Kinloch*.

In 1879 *Gael* was fitted with a deck saloon aft and a new boiler was fitted. In April 1884 she was sold to the Great Western Railway, and was initially used by them from Weymouth to Cherbourg. In the summers from 1884 until 1886 she operated excursions on the Bristol Channel from Portishead to Ilfracombe and from 1888 to 1889 ran from Penzance to the Scilly Isles on charter to the West Cornwall Steamship Co. Ltd. In 1891 she was sold to David MacBrayne for service out of Oban. In 1917 she was chartered to the Caledonian Steam Packet Co. to replace some of their steamers, which were on war service. Early 1919 saw her on charter to the GSWR for the Arran service. She was scrapped in 1924. The view above shows her in colours off Kyle of Lochalsh, with with the wooden whaleback focsle, which was added for her service from Weymouth.

Kintyre was built in 1868 by Robertson & Co. with two-cylinder simple expansion engines by Blackwood & Gordon and is seen her at Carradale. In 1882 she was fitted with new compound machinery by Kincaid, Donald, & Co. She maintained the year-round cargo and passenger service from a river berth at Glasgow to Lochranza, Pirnmill, Carradale, and Campbeltown. On 18 September 1907 she was on a light run from Glasgow to Campbeltown to take sheep to Tarbert. She was run down and sunk of Skelmorlie by the Union SS of New Zealand's new *Maori*, which was on builder's trials, as the latter wan making a U-turn at the top of the measured mile. The wreck of *Kintyre* is today a popular site for divers.

Kinloch, seen here leaving Campbeltown, was built in 1878 by A&J Inglis and was a larger version of *Kintyre* and built with compound machinery.

Kinloch off Gourock. She normally ran along with *Kintyre*, with one steamer leaving Campbeltown and one leaving Glasgow each day for the single journey.

Kinloch in the River Clyde passing Rothesay Dock in August 1923. She was withdrawn in May 1926 when replaced by *Dalriada* and was sold to the Channel Islands Packet Co. Ltd for excursions from Jersey to St Malo, Granville and Sark. She was sold two years later for breaking up at Bo'ness. (*A. Ernest Glen collection*)

Davaar was built in 1885 at the yard of the London & Glasgow Iron Shipbuilding Co. Ltd at Govan which she is seen passing here in a unique illustration. She was fitted with compound machinery and was originally fitted with two funnels as seen here in a postcard view in the River Clyde. She initially replaced *Gael* on the run from Greenock.

Davaar in two-funnelled condition arriving at Lochranza in a postcard view.

Davaar also operated some excursions, sailing on a two-day trip to Douglas, Isle of Man in 1885, Fort William in September 1894, and Oban in September 1895 and for the following three years. An annual day trip to Belfast had been operated by the company since 1828 and was operated by *Davaar* on 7 June 1895, on which date she ran aground on Briggs Reef off the southern shore of Belfast Lough. All the passengers were landed safely by the ship's lifeboats and she was pulled off on 9 June and resumed service on the 12th of that month. (*A. Ernest Glen collection*)

The Highlander figurehead of *Davaar* in her late 1930s condition. (*A. Ernest Glen collection*)

In the 1902-1903 winter *Davaar* was reboilered and emerged with a single funnel. At the same time her aft saloon was extended the full width of the hull and to the stern.

From 1908 for a spell *Davaar* operated a daily return sailing to Campbeltown, leaving Glasgow Broomielaw at 06.00, and calling at Princes Pier and Gourock, returning to Glasgow at 21.30. She is seen here arriving at Carradale.

Davaar arriving at Gourock in October 1928. On 4 March 1937 the Clyde and Campbeltown Company amalgamated with Clyde Cargo Steamers Ltd and the combined company became the Clyde & Campbeltown Shipping Co., partly owned by David MacBrayne Ltd. From midsummer of that year the funnels were repainted in the MacBrayne colours. *(A. Ernest Glen collection)*

Davaar at Campbeltown between 1937 and 1939 with a red and black funnel with *Glen Sannox* berthed across the end of the pier. (A. Ernest Glen Collection)

Davaar in the River Clyde off Erskine. On 2 October 1939 *Davaar* performed what was scheduled to be her last passenger sailing and was laid up in East India Harbour, Greenock. The company had announced the withdrawal of the passenger service in August of that year. This was due to declining traffic and not the imminent outbreak of war. From 9 January until 15 March 1940 *Davaar* was again on the service, now running from Wemyss Bay. In July of that year she was requisitioned by the Admiralty for possible use as a blockship at Newhaven. She was moored inside the harbour entrance with steam up ready to sail out and be sunk at the entrance in the event of a German invasion. In July 1943 she was beached ¼ mile east of the harbour and was dismantled.

Dalriada was built in 1926 by R. Duncan & Co. Ltd as a centenary steamer to replace *Kinloch*. She had four-cylinder triple-expansion machinery by D. Rowan & Co. Ltd and was to be the fastest single screw steamer in the world, with a speed of 17 knots. On 30 April 1926 she made the run from Gourock to Campbeltown in the record time of two hours forty-five minutes.

Dalriada off Tighnabruiach in 1926, on a special sailing round Bute.

Dalriada at Lochranza. Note that the bow plating is now painted black.

Dalriada approaching Carradale northbound, from a postcard view.

Dalriada dressed overall for the Silver Jubilee of King George V in 1935.

Dalriada in mid-firth.

SATURDAY AFTERNOON
EXCURSIONS

—TO—

Lochranza, Pirnmill, Carradale & Campbeltown

From JUNE 30th to AUGUST 25th (Except 14th JULY)

BY R.M.S.

"DALRIADA" & "DAVAAR"

Trains from GLASGOW and PAISLEY

CENTRAL STATION to GOUROCK	**- - 1-5 p.m.**
ST. ENOCH STATION to PRINCES PIER	**- 12-41 p.m.**
PAISLEY (Gilmour St.) to GOUROCK	**- 12-59 p.m.**
Do. (do.) to PRINCES PIER	**12-55 p.m.**

From PRINCES PIER, 1-40 p.m.; GOUROCK, 2-0 p.m.

Returning from

CAMPBELTOWN 6-15 p.m.

Allowing about 4 hours ashore at	LOCHRANZA
,, ,, 3 ,, ,,	PIRNMILL
,, ,, 2½ ,, ,,	CARRADALE
,, ,, ¾ ,, ,,	CAMPBELTOWN

RETURN FARES:

From GLASGOW and PAISLEY	3rd Class and Cabin.	3rd Class and Steerage.
To LOCHRANZA & PIRNMILL -	**5/8**	**4/-**
,, CARRADALE & CAMPBELTOWN	**6/8**	**5/-**

	STEAMER ONLY.	
From PRINCES PIER and GOUROCK	Cabin.	Steerage.
To LOCHRANZA and PIRNMILL - - -	**4/-**	**2/4**
,, CARRADALE and CAMPBELTOWN - -	**5/-**	**3/4**

CAMPBELTOWN & GLASGOW STEAM PACKET JOINT STOCK CO., LTD., 5 Bridge Wharf, Glasgow.

Telephone : 4307 Central.   1/6/34.

John Horn, Ltd.. Glasgow and London.

A summer 1934 handbill for afternoon excursions to Lochranza, Pirnmill, Carradale and Campbeltown by *Davaar* and *Dalriada*.

CHEAP DAY EXCURSIONS

On MONDAYS and SATURDAYS

From 3rd JULY until 30th AUGUST
(Except SATURDAY, 17th JULY, and MONDAY, 26th JULY)

TO

LOCHRANZA, PIRNMILL, CARRADALE

AND

CAMPBELTOWN

BY R.M.S.

"DALRIADA" & "DAVAAR"

Trains from GLASGOW and PAISLEY :

CENTRAL STATION to GOUROCK ... ... 8.35 a.m.

ST. ENOCH STATION to PRINCES PIER ... ... 7.30 a.m.

PAISLEY (Gilmour St.) to GOUROCK ... ... 8.47 a.m.

PAISLEY (Gilmour St.) to PRINCES PIER ... ... 7.47 a.m.

From Princes Pier 9.0 a.m., Gourock 9.30 a.m.

Returning from CAMPBELTOWN—Mondays 3.30 p.m., Saturdays 6.15 p.m.

ALLOWING PASSENGERS THE UNDERNOTED TIMES ASHORE :

				Mondays.	Saturdays.
LOCHRANZA	...	...	...	6 hours	8 hours
PIRNMILL	...	...	...	5 ,,	7 ,,
CARRADALE	...	...	...	4 ,,	6 ,,
CAMPBELTOWN	...	...	...	2 ,,	4 ,,

RETURN FARES :

From GLASGOW and PAISLEY.	1st Class and Cabin.	3rd Class and Cabin.	3rd Class & Steerage.
To **LOCHRANZA & PIRNMILL** ...	7/6	6/8	5/2
,, **CARRADALE & CAMPBELTOWN**	8/6	7/8	5/8

	STEAMER ONLY.	
From PRINCES PIER and GOUROCK.	Cabin.	Steerage.
To **LOCHRANZA and PIRNMILL**	5/-	3/6
,, **CARRADALE and CAMPBELTOWN**	6/-	4/-

CLYDE & CAMPBELTOWN SHIPPING CO., LTD.,
171-175 Clyde Street, Glasgow.

Telephone—973 Central.   July, 1937.

GLASGOW **JOHN HORN** LONDON
LIMITED

A summer 1937 handbill, this time by the Clyde and Campbeltown Shipping Co. Ltd for cheap day excursions to Lochranza, Pirnmill, Carradale and Campbeltown by *Davaar* and *Dalriada*. (*CRSC Archive*)

A busy *Dalriada* departing from Gourock, in the MacBrayne funnel period from 1937 to 1939. In the background a Kelly coaster can be seen en route to Ireland.

Dalriada maintained the Campbeltown service alone from 2 October 1939. From the middle of that month her funnel was painted black and a few days later her saloon was also painted black. She is seen here at Wemyss Bay on 1 January 1940. On 7 January 1940 she was struck off Campbeltown by a destroyer and was withdrawn from service and laid up in the East India Harbour at Greenock. In April 1941 she was requisitioned for use as a salvage vessel on the Thames. She was sunk by a mine in the Edinburgh Channel of the River Thames on 19 June 1942, and in June 1946 the wreck was blown up to clear the channel.

Three
Clyde Cargo Steamers

The first *Bute* was built by Scott's of Bowling in 1879. She was wrecked in 1891 while on a special run from Islay to Liverpool. (*G.E. Langmuir Collection, Mitchell Library*)

In 1882, on the opening of Fairlie Pier, Hill & Co. went into the passenger business from there to Millport with *Cumbrae*, seen here leaving Keppel Pier. She had been built in 1863 by Barclay Curle, with a single cylinder steeple engine by J. Barr, as *Victory* for Capt. Duncan Stewart for the Glasgow to Rothesay run. She was sold after a year to the Wemyss Bay Railway Co. In 1871 she was sold to Duncan Dewar and renamed *Marquis of Lorne*, becoming a 'Sunday-breaker'. She was sold in 1888 and became a coal hulk at Newry in 1892.

Opposite: Hill & Co. were the major contributor to the fleet of Clyde Cargo Steamers when the latter company was founded in 1915. Their first steamer was *Success*, which replaced a sailing vessel of the same name, and was built in 1876 by Murdoch & Murray with two-cylinder simple expansion machinery by Kesson & Campbell. She served alongside *Bute* but was sold in 1882. (*G.E. Langmuir Collection, Mitchell Library*)

A second paddle steamer was purchased for the Millport service in 1883. *Arran*, seen here off Arrochar, had also been a 'Sunday-breaker' and had been built as *Dunoon Castle* in 1867 by T. Wingate & Co. for the Dunoon & Rothesay Carriers, who attempted to set up their own steamer service. In 1871 she was sold, and again in 1874 to Henry Sharp. At that stage she had a second funnel. In 1884 Hill sold her to Gillies & Campbell for the Wemyss Bay to Rothesay service. She was sold off the river and operated on the Mersey in 1885, on the Thames in 1891, and latterly on the Shannon as a tug, before being scrapped in 1896.

Bute No.2 was built in 1890 by Scott's of Bowling, and was intended to carry both cargo and passengers. The advent of the Glasgow & South Western Railway Steamers in 1891 made her service uneconomic, and she was sold to Venezuelan owners, being renamed *Higuerote* and later *Ossun*. Her name was written as such because at the time she was built, *Bute* of 1879, was still in service. She is seen here at the Albert Pier in Rothesay with *Marquis of Bute* arriving and *Sultan* at the pier. (*G.E. Langmuir collection, Mitchell Library*)

A third *Bute* was built in 1892 by J. Fullerton & Co. of Paisley. In 1901 she was sold to Glasgow Steam Coasters and renamed *Dunard*, and was later sold on to other owners. *(G.E. Langmuir collection, Mitchell Library)*

Bute 4, seen here off Yoker, was built by Fullerton of Paisley in 1898, and served Hill & Co. and later Clyde Cargo Steamers until broken up at Ardrossan in 1935.

Bute 4 entering Kingston Dock in March 1926. *(A. Ernest Glen collection)*

Bute 4 arriving at Rothesay, Albert Pier.

The final steamer to be purchased by Hill & Co. was the second *Arran*. She had been built as a steam yacht named *Barmore* by Fullerton's in 1879, and had been converted to a cargo vessel by an Orkney owner who purchased her in 1911. In 1912 Hill & Co. purchased her, and she served them until sold in August 1917 to a Glasgow fish merchant.

The Lochfyne & Glasgow Steam Packet Co. owed its origins to the Jura Steamboat Co., which operated *Jura* on cargo services to that island. She was built in 1869 at Dumbarton and served until April 1913. (*G.E. Langmuir Collection, Mitchell Library*)

Minard Castle was built in 1882 by Fullerton of Paisley, with compound machinery by W. Kemp, for the Lochfyne & Glasgow Steam Packet Co. to operate a cargo service from Glasgow to the Loch Fyne ports in opposition to MacBraynes. In 1913 she was taken over by R.G. Campbell and shortly after was registered as belonging to the Minard Castle Shipping Co. Ltd. In 1915 she came under the ownership of Clyde Cargo Steamers Ltd. She is seen here at Inveraray pier. (*A. Ernest Glen Collection*)

Minard Castle laid up at Bowling in May 1926. She was sold for scrapping at Port Glasgow in November of that year. In 1899 the Lochfyne & Glasgow Steam Packet Co. purchased the paddle steamer *Sultana* and ran her on a service from Kingston Dock to Ardrishaig via Dunoon, Fairlie, Millport, Skipness and Tarbert. This was one of the few scheduled calls ever for passengers by a Clyde steamer at Skipness Pier. (*Robin Boyd Collection*)

The first purchase of Clyde Cargo Steamers Ltd was MacBrayne's *Lapwing*, which entered service in 1918. She had been built in 1903 by Scotts of Bowling, with machinery by Hutson & Sons Ltd, and had run aground near Oban in 1916 and been taken over by the underwriters. She was taken over by the Admiralty shortly after entering service for Clyde Cargo Steamers and operated from Penzance to the Scilly Islands, and later from Plymouth to the Channel Islands. She is seen here departing from Penzance.

Lapwing returned to the Clyde in 1920 and was renamed *Cowal* in 1926. She was scrapped at Troon in 1932. She is seen here in August 1925 passing Water's Neb on the River Clyde. (*A. Ernest Glen Collection*)

George Brown & Co. of Greenock had built *Lintie* in 1909 for the tug-owners Steel & Bennie, who operated a cargo service with her from Glasgow to Greenock. She had a very short funnel to pass above Glasgow Bridge. She was purchased by Clyde Cargo Steamers along with her trade in 1925 and was sold soon afterwards to an owner at Belfast. She is seen here in the Kingston Dock. (*G.E. Langmuir Collection, Mitchell Library*)

Opposite: Jane was a former trawler which had been built by the Ardrossan Dockyard Co. in 1901. She was purchased in 1924 by Clyde Cargo Steamers with the aim of providing en express service to Rothesay but was sold in April 1926. She is seen here at Alloa in 1932 with the paddle box of the former GSWR steamer *Juno*, which was then being broken up there. (*G.E. Langmuir Collection, Mitchell Library*)

A third *Arran*, seen here leaving Bowling Harbour, was built in 1926. She was built by the Ayrshire Dockyard Co. Ltd, with machinery by Aitchison Blair, and replaced *Jane* in the fleet. She ran mainly to Arran and Skipness, and occasionally to Loch Fyne. In January 1933, whilst on the latter service, she was wrecked on Barmore Island where MacBrayne's *Chevalier* had met her end some six years earlier.

Minard was built in 1925 by Scotts of Bowling with engines by Aitchison Blair Ltd of Clydebank. She mainly served on the Glasgow to Loch Fyne run and, after the war, on the Glasgow to Rothesay cargo service. She is seen here in July 1934 with white lifeboats. (*Robin Boyd Collection*)

Minard off Gourock in 1946, now with a red and black MacBrayne funnel carried from 1937 to 1949. (*Robin Boyd Collection*)

Minard in Kingston Dock post-1949 with yellow and black British Railways funnel. Her service ceased on 1 October 1954 after the introduction of the car ferry service from Wemyss Bay and *Minard* was withdrawn and scrapped at Port Glasgow in the following year along with the paddle steamer *Marchioness of Lorne* (1935). (*Robin Boyd Collection*)

Ardyne, seen here in Rothesay Bay, came in 1928, also from Scotts of Bowling. She was similar to *Minard* but slightly shorter. She operated on the Campbeltown cargo run from the withdrawal of *Davaar* in March 1940 until it was closed on 31 October 1949. She became spare steamer and was sold in April 1955 to a Belfast owner, but went for scrapping at Troon in autumn 1955. (*A. Ernest Glen collection*)

Ardyne across the end of the pier at Rothesay.

The final steamer to be built for Clyde Cargo Steamers was a fourth *Arran*, this one coming from the Ardrossan Dockyard in 1933, again with machinery by Aitchison Blair. In post-war years she was on the Ardrossan to Arran and Millport service taking the place of *Arran Mail*. (*Robin Boyd Collection*)

In 1952 *Arran* was renamed *Kildonan* and was withdrawn after the car ferry *Glen Sannox* entered service in 1957. She was sold for scrapping at Port Glasgow in the following year. She is seen here off Brodick. (*Robin Boyd*)

CLYDE COAST, ARRAN, LOCH FYNE AND CAMPBELTOWN STEAMERS

"ARDYNE" "ARRAN" "DALRIADA" "DAVAAR" "MINARD"
or other Steamers

MARCH, 1937 (until further Notice)

The following Cargo Steamer Services will be given from **GLASGOW and GREENOCK** (weather and circumstances permitting), calling at the following places, viz.:—

From Sheds Nos. 1 and 2, KINGSTON DOCK, GLASGOW, about 6 a.m.

TO

ARDRISHAIG -	Daily.	Kilmun -	- Tuesday, Thursday and Saturday.
Auchenlochan -	Daily.	Kirn -	- Daily.
Blairmore -	Tuesday, Thursday and Saturday.	Lamlash -	- Tuesday, Thursday and Saturday.
BRODICK -	Tuesday, Thursday and Saturday.	MILLPORT -	Tuesday, Thursday and Saturday.
Colintraive -	Daily.	Ormidale -	- Wednesday—Inward Tuesday.
Cove -	- Tuesday, Thursday and Saturday.	Otter Ferry -	Tuesday, Thursday and Saturday.
Crarae -	Tuesday, Thursday and Saturday.	ROTHESAY -	Daily Express Direct Service at 2 a.m. also Daily from Greenock about 9 a.m.
DUNOON -	Daily Express Direct Service, except Monday, at 4 a.m., Monday at 2 a.m., also Daily from Greenock about 9 a.m.		
		Sandbank-	Tuesday, Thursday and Saturday.
Furnace -	- Tuesday, Thursday and Saturday.	Strachur -	Tuesday, Thursday and Saturday.
Hunter's Quay	Tuesday, Thursday and Saturday.	Strone -	- Tuesday, Thursday and Saturday.
Innellan -	- Daily.	TARBERT -	Daily.
Inveraray -	Tuesday, Thursday and Saturday.	Tighnabruaich -	Daily.
Kilchattan Bay	Tuesday, Thursday and Saturday.		
Kilcreggan -	Tuesday, Thursday and Saturday.	Whiting Bay -	Tuesday, Thursday and Saturday.

From Shed No. 5, BRIDGE WHARF, GLASGOW
Daily except Mondays at 6 a.m. (Mondays from Greenock only)
TO
LOCHRANZA, PIRNMILL, CARRADALE and CAMPBELTOWN

The FREIGHT of all GOODS must be paid at Shipment for the undernoted places, viz.:—
COLINTRAIVE, ORMIDALE, TIGHNABRUAICH, AUCHENLOCHAN, SKIPNESS, OTTER FERRY.
CRARAE, FURNACE, STRACHUR, LOCHRANZA, PIRNMILL and CARRADALE.

ROAD TRANSPORT GOODS SERVICE
FROM
GLASGOW, 171 Clyde Street (Custom House Quay), at 6.0 a.m. and 10.30 a.m. daily, and at 12.30 p.m. on Tuesday, Wednesday, Thursday and Friday
TO
Luss, Tarbet, Arrochar, Cairndow, Inveraray, Furnace, Crarae, Minard, Lochgair, Lochgilphead and Ardrishaig, with connecting Services to Kilmartin and Ford.
TO
Tarbert at 10.30 a.m. daily.
TO
Cairnbaan, Bellanoch and Crinan at 6 a.m. on Wednesday and Friday.
Goods should be addressed and consigned *PER ROAD SERVICE.*
All Goods conveyed by above Motor Service are covered by the usual Insurance against loss and damage.

For further particulars apply to Agents at above places, or to

CLYDE AND CAMPBELTOWN SHIPPING COY. LTD.
171-175 CLYDE STREET (Custom House Quay), GLASGOW, C.1
(Telephone Central 973 Private Branch Exchange)
(Telegraphic Address "Coastwards, Glasgow")

and CUSTOMS HOUSE QUAY, GREENOCK

Cargo for Shipment to be delivered alongside Steamers not later than 5 p.m.

A poster advertising the cargo services of the Clyde & Campbeltown Shipping Co. in March 1937 with *Ardyne*, *Arran*, *Dalriada*, *Davaar*, and *Minard*.

Marie, seen here leaving Dunoon showing the buoy, since removed, marking the shallow water approach, was a small fish-carrying steamer purchased in 1939 by the Clyde & Campbeltown Shipping Co., but which had been chartered by them on occasion previously. She had been built by W. Chalmers & Co. at Rutherglen in 1904 with machinery by Ross & Duncan and was sold to Norwegian owners in 1949.

Empire Tulip was chartered from the Ministry of Transport in 1945 and 1946 for the cargo run to Campbeltown. She had been Dutch-built in 1939. (*G E Langmuir Collection, Mitchell Library*)

Four
Miscellaneous Vessels

Adela was the last flush-decked paddle steamer to be built for service on the Clyde when she was built in 1877 by Caird & Co. of Greenock for Gillies & Campbell. She remained in their fleet on the Wemyss Bay to Rothesay service until 1889.

Adela arriving at Rothesay. In summer 1890 she offered sailings from Southport, and the following year she was sold to the Brighton, Worthing, & South Coast Steamboat Co. She served them as *Sea Breeze* until sold to owners at Marseilles in 1896. They renamed her *La Corse*, and she was scrapped in 1898.

The two-funnelled saloon steamer *Victoria*, seen between Craigmore and Rothesay, was built in 1886 by Blackwood & Gordon for Gillies & Campbell's services from Wemyss Bay. In 1890 her owners gave in to the competition from the railway steamers and she operated on charter on Belfast Lough for that season after a brief interlude from Liverpool to Llandudno. In 1891 she was chartered to operate from Swansea, but in 1892 came back to the Clyde to sail for The Scottish Excursion Steamer Co. Ltd on a Fairlie to Campbeltown run. In September 1893 she caught fire whilst lying at the Broomielaw and was sold in May of the next year for service on the Thames. In 1894 she ran from Great Yarmouth to Harwich.

Victoria came back to the Clyde in 1897 and sailed for The Clyde Steamers Ltd, owned by Dawson Reid, running from Glasgow to Skipness via the Kyles of Bute. On Sundays she sailed round Bute, Inchmarnock, and Cumbrae. She is seen here at Auchenlochan. In this period she was involved in a riot at Dunoon when her passengers tried to force their way onto the pier, which was closed on Sundays, although on most Sundays during that summer passengers were landed at Dunoon by means of the steamer's lifeboats.

Victoria, seen here leaving Craigmore, left the Clyde in 1898, replaced by *Duchess of York*, ex *Jeanie Deans*. She returned to the Thames until 1900 and was then scrapped.

Culzean Castle had been built in 1891 at Southampton as *Windsor Castle* for the Bournemouth & South Coast Steam Packet Co. Ltd. She was sold to the Glasgow, Ayrshire & Campbeltown Steamboat Co. in 1895 to replace *Victoria* on the Campbeltown excursion, this time sailing from Greenock rather than Fairlie. She is seen here in 1895 condition, with a yellow funnel and two masts. She was not successful in that year and sailed on only 4 days. This is one of only two photographs known to have been taken of her in that year. She offered this service until 1897, with calls at Dunoon, Largs, Fairlie, Millport (Keppel), Lochranza, Pirnmill and Machrie Bay. She was the first Clyde steamer to have triple expansion three-crank machinery.

Culzean Castle offered upriver excursions after the 1897 season, and was renamed *Carrick Castle* in 1899. In 1900 she was sold to the Russian Government and ended her career in Japanese waters as *Tenri Maru*.

Fairy was a tiny paddle steamer, probably more aptly described as a paddle launch, which offered a ferry service across Loch Fyne from Inveraray to St Catherine's, where she is seen here. She was built in 1893, replacing a predecessor of the same name, and served the route until replaced by a motorboat in 1913.

OFF TO AILSA CRAIG, GIRVAN 1341.

A. S. Girvan of Girvan ran trips from Girvan to Ailsa Craig to land at the pier there with *Ailsa* of 1906. She was built in Troon by the Ailsa Shipbuilding Co. and served on the route until sold in 1924 to Cromarty owners for a Cromarty to Invergordon service. In 1938 she was sold to owners in Orkney for service to Burray and North Ronaldsay.

Ailsa leaving Girvan for Ailsa Craig. She was succeeded by *Ailsa II*, built in 1924 by Ailsa Shipbuilding at Ayr, and renamed *Lady Ailsa* shortly after her introduction. She was sold to French owners in 1932, and replaced by a converted fishing boat of the same name.

Lady Ailsa is seen here at the landing jetty at Ailsa Craig. (*G.E. Langmuir Collection, Mitchell Library*)

In 1920 the firm of T.L. Duff & Co. advertised the Anchor Line tender *Skirmisher* for charters on the Clyde. The Anchor Line's other tender, *Paladin*, also ran excursions from Glasgow to Dunoon.

The wooden-hulled paddle yacht *Comet* was built in 1892 by Archibald Rodger of Port Glasgow for H. McIntyre, and designed by the latter. McIntyre had had a shipyard at Paisley until 1885, his last steamer built here being *Waverley* for P&A Campbell. In the July and August of 1893 she offered cruises every two or three hours from Rothesay to Loch Striven, with landing advertised, and to the Kyles of Bute and Loch Riddon. On 7 March 1894 she was destroyed by fire at McIntyre's Kelliebank shipyard at Alloa, where he later built *Cambria* for P&A Campbell. She was not the only paddle yacht advertised to offer excursions from Rothesay in that summer, *Erne* and *Greenan Castle* offered cruises at the beginning of July, the former to view the regatta, and the latter to the Kyles of Bute. (G.E. Langmuir Collection, Mitchell Library)

Other small boats operating out of Rothesay have included *Gay Queen* of 1938, which offered short cruises until sold to Poole in 1983, where she was renamed *Anne Marie* and remains in service at the time of writing.

Maid of Bute, seen here in a postcard view passing the Albert Pier at Rothesay with *Queen Mary II* and *Maid of Argyll* at the steamer pier, offered similar trips from Rothesay. In the sixties she was occasionally chartered by the CSP for an evening Tighnabruiach run when *Countess of Breadalbane*, the usual vessel on this service, was not available. She was sold in 1973 to an owner at Fort William, and after that to owners at South Queensferry and at Southend on Sea.

In 1948 the Belfast tender *Duchess of Abercorn*, built by Harland & Wolff at Belfast in 1936, appeared on the Clyde for the Mac Shipping Co. Ltd renamed *Wimaisia*. She offered a service from Bridge Wharf to Campbeltown, where she is seen here with *Duchess of Montrose*, in a photograph taken from *Marchioness of Graham*. This was advertised as for first class passengers and light luggage. From 21 July of that year this service was offered from Ardrossan rather than Glasgow and from August she called at Whiting Bay rather than Lochranza. She was sold in October 1948 to Liverpool for use as a fireboat.

Glasgow–Campbeltown Passenger Service

T.S.M.V. "Wimaisia"

Times of sailing :—

Glasgow (Bridge Wharf)		8.00 a.m.
Bowling		9.00 a.m.
Greenock (Custom House Quay)		10.00 a.m.
Lochranza		12.30 p.m.
Campbeltown ...	arr.	2.30 p.m.
Campbeltown ...	dep.	3.00 p.m.
Lochranza		5.00 p.m.
Greenock (Custom House Quay)		7:30 p.m.
Bowling		8.00 p.m.
Glasgow (Bridge Wharf)		9.00 p.m.

Service will run :—

Daily from 29th June to 6th September
Friday to Mon. inclusive from 10th Sept. to 27th Sept.

There will be sailings on Sundays

MEALS ON BOARD AT RESTAURANT CHARGES

FARES

Glasgow / Campbeltown	Return 20 –	Single 13 4
Glasgow / Lochranza	Return 17 6	Single 12 6

An advertisement featuring the 1948 timetable for *Wimaisia*.

Wimaisia was joined by the former yacht *Taransay*, seen here off the John Brown yard at Clydebank, which carried cargo and a few third class passengers from Glasgow Princes Dock to Campbeltown. She was sold to the Wimaisia Shipping Co. Ltd in April 1949 and was sold for scrapping at Port Glasgow in 1955.

In 1950 the Fairmile launch *Ulster Lady* ran one season of cruises from Greenock's Princes Pier to Rothesay with short cruises from Rothesay. She had previously run on the Forth and Tay as *Royal Tay Lady* and *Tay Lady*, and from Belfast as *Ulster Lady*. After the 1950 season she returned to Granton and was laid up for some years before being broken up. *Queen Mary II* can be seen in the background.

In 1965 a hovercraft service was operated on the Clyde by Clyde Hover Ferries Ltd with two Westland SRN6 vessels. The main service was from Largs to Millport, operating from beach locations at each place.

Later in the year a service was advertised from Tarbert to Gourock, and a commuter service operated from Dunoon to Gourock and Craigendoran. The service was short-lived and ceased by the end of the year.

In 1974 Sir Robert McAlpine & Sons Ltd purchased the Bournemouth excursion vessel, *Bournemouth Queen*, for a workmen's service from Rothesay to their oil rig construction yard at Ardyne. She had been built as *Coronia* in 1935 for excursions from Scarborough, and had been sold to Croson's of Poole in 1966 to replace the paddle steamer *Embassy*.

In June 1975 *Bournemouth Queen* was renamed *Queen of Scots* and, for a few weeks in summer 1977, was chartered to Waverley Steam Navigation Co. Ltd as a very useful back up for *Waverley*, which had grounded on the Gantocks off Dunoon on 15 July. She is seen here departing Millport with *Waverley* at the pier at the conclusion of this service on 1 September, having transferred stores, etc. to *Waverley*.

In 1978 *Queen of Scots* was purchased by BB Shipping Co. and operated excursions from Princes Dock, as seen here.

Queen of Scots arriving at Gourock in 1978. Her lack of speed and of covered accommodation conspired against her and she lasted a few seasons on excursions. She was then laid up for a long spell at Blairmore, and was eventually sold for conversion to a floating restaurant on the River Medway.

Clyde Marine Motoring Co. Ltd have operated *Rover* since her building at Renfrew in 1964 on excursions and charters in the Firth of Clyde from their Gourock base.